WORDS, SONGS, AND ACTIVITIES
BY
ERIC H.F. LAW

DOODLES IN THE MARGINS
BY
DAVE LAW

chalice
press

Saint Louis, Missouri

An imprint of Christian Board of Publication

CONTENTS

IN MEMORY OF
PARENTS/GRANDPARENTS:

LAW KWOK-NAM
FOR PASSING ON THE
CREATIVE GENES TO US,

AND

LAW TAM UN-OI
FOR GIVING US THE
SPIRIT OF KINDNESS AND GENEROSITY.

FOR ELLIO AND CLAIRE
YOU ARE BLESSINGS
AND YOU ARE BLESSED
SO BE WELL, CREATE AND GIVE.

HEY, WELCOME!

THIS IS NOT A **BOOK** THAT YOU JUST READ. THIS IS A **BOOK** THAT YOU DO. IT CONTAINS 52 WEEKS OF ACTIVITIES, AND WHEN YOU DO THEM FAITHFULLY, YOU WILL BECOME AN **AWESOME, AMAZING** AND **ANIMATED** STEWARD OF **GOD'S** CREATION.

YOU WILL BE AN **AWESOME** STEWARD BECAUSE WHAT YOU **GIVE** AND **RECEIVE** IS NOT JUST MONEY BUT ALSO RELATIONSHIP, TRUTH, TIME, PLACE, GRACIOUS LEADERSHIP AND WELLNESS!

YOU WILL BE AN **AMAZING** STEWARD BECAUSE YOU KNOW WHO YOU ARE, WHAT YOU HAVE, **WHERE** YOU HAVE INFLUENCE, AND **WHAT** YOU ARE WILLING TO **GIVE** AND **RECEIVE** TO FOSTER **WELLNESS** FOR YOURSELF, YOUR COMMUNITY, AND THE EARTH.

YOU WILL BE AN **ANIMATED** STEWARD BECAUSE YOU ARE USING YOUR WHOLE BEING IN DOING THESE ACTIVITIES - READING, WRITING, DRAWING, LISTENING, IMAGINING, MEDITATING, SINGING, DANCING, SEEING REALITY, SPEAKING TRUTH, HUGGING FRIENDS, WALKING THE NEIGHBOR-HOOD, SHAKING HANDS WITH NEIGHBORS, FACING ENEMIES, AND BLESSING PLACES.

FOR AN EVEN MORE **AWESOME** EXPERIENCE, GATHER A GROUP OF FIVE TO EIGHT FRIENDS AND COMMIT TO ENGAGING THIS BOOK FOR THE **YEAR.** MEET WEEKLY OR MONTHLY TO SHARE PROGRESS. USE THE GRACIOUS LEADERSHIP SKILLS FROM WEEK 12 AND 13 TO FACILITATE THE SHARING. REMEMBER TO TELL YOUR CHURCH LEADERSHIP WHAT YOU ARE UP TO SO THEY WON'T BE SURPRISED WHEN **AWESOME** AND **AMAZING** THINGS ARE HAPPENING.

TO GAIN A DEEPER UNDERSTANDING OF THE **SIX CURRENCIES,** READ THE OTHER TWO **HOLY CURRENCY** BOOKS:

HOLY CURRENCIES: 6 BLESSINGS FOR SUSTAINABLE AND MISSIONAL MINISTRIES

HOLY CURRENCY EXCHANGE: 101 STORIES, SONGS, ACTIONS AND VISIONS OF MISSIONAL AND SUSTAINABLE MINISTRIES

YOU CAN PURCHASE THEM FROM THE PUBLISHER, *CHALICE PRESS,* OR ANY-WHERE BOOKS ARE SOLD.

FINALLY, REGISTER AT WWW.HOLYCURRENCIES.COM TO GET ADDITIONAL AWESOME STUFF TO MAKE THIS AN EVEN MORE AMAZING YEAR.

ERIC & DAVE

WEEK 1

☐ I CHOSE TO BUY THIS BOOK BECAUSE...
☐ I WAS GIVEN THIS BOOK BECAUSE...

_____
_____
_____

☐ I PAID $_____ FOR THIS BOOK
☐ THIS BOOK IS A GIFT FROM

_____

COMPLETE THE PLEDGE CARD ON THIS PAGE. FIND AN ACCOUNTABLE
PERSON TO SIGN IT. TAKE A PHOTO AND SEND IT TO SOMEONE WHO OVERSEES
STEWARDSHIP MINISTRY IN YOUR CHURCH.

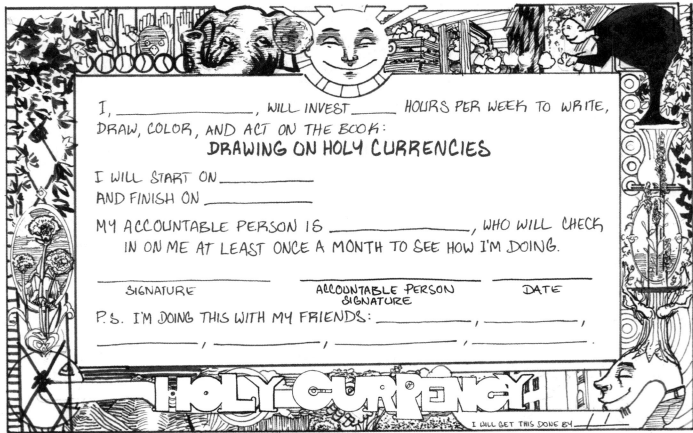

I, _____, WILL INVEST _____ HOURS PER WEEK TO WRITE,
DRAW, COLOR, AND ACT ON THE BOOK:
DRAWING ON HOLY CURRENCIES

I WILL START ON _____
AND FINISH ON _____

MY ACCOUNTABLE PERSON IS _____, WHO WILL CHECK
  IN ON ME AT LEAST ONCE A MONTH TO SEE HOW I'M DOING.

_____   _____   _____
SIGNATURE   ACCOUNTABLE PERSON   DATE
                           SIGNATURE
P.S. I'M DOING THIS WITH MY FRIENDS: _____, _____,
_____, _____, _____.

HOLY CURRENCY

I WILL GET THIS DONE BY ___/___/___

FEEL FREE TO COLOR THIS PAGE BEFORE YOU SEND IT.

I HOPE THE EXCHANGES FOR READING, WRITING, COLORING, ACTING, AND DRAWING ON THIS BOOK WILL BE...

_____

_____

_____

_____

(COME BACK AND ADD TO THIS AS YOU DISCOVER NEW EXCHANGES.)

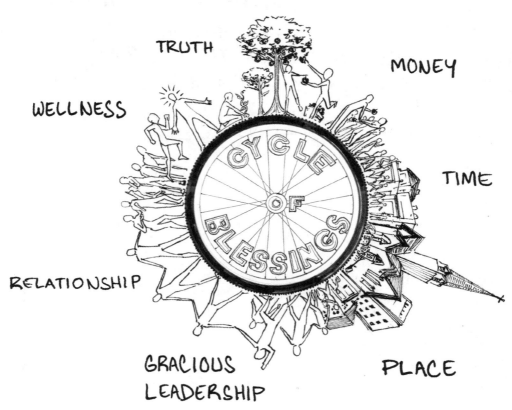

TRUTH

MONEY

WELLNESS

TIME

RELATIONSHIP

GRACIOUS LEADERSHIP

PLACE

REGISTER AT WWW.HOLYCURRENCIES.COM AND GET A PASSWORD TO ACCESS OTHER COOL HOLY CURRENCY STUFF LIKE VIDEOS, SONGS, LINKS DRAWINGS, ETC.

LISTEN TO ERIC H.F. LAW'S VERSION OF *PRAISE GOD FROM WHOM ALL BLESSINGS FLOW* AT WWW.HOLYCURRENCIES.COM
AS YOU COLOR THE NEXT PAGE, LOOK FOR AND HIGHLIGHT THE FOLLOWING TEXT:

PRAISE GOD FROM WHOM ALL BLESSINGS FLOW
CIRCLING THROUGH EARTH SO ALL MY GROW
VANQUISHING FEAR SO ALL MAY GIVE
WIDENING GRACE SO ALL MAY LIVE

SING AND MEDITATE ON THESE WORDS AS YOU COLOR. FEEL FREE TO ADD MORE WORDS TO THE PICTURE IF YOU ARE SO INSPIRED. WHEN YOU'RE DONE, TAKE A PHOTO OF IT AND POST IT ON INSTAGRAM, FACEBOOK, TWITTER, ETC. WITH #HOLYCURRENCIES.

MY NAME IS: _____

THE STORY OR MEANING OF MY NAME (WRITE OR DRAW):

IF YOU DON'T KNOW IT, FIND OUT ... OR MAKE IT UP.

I AM A GIFT FROM _____

I AM A GIFT FOR _____

COMPLETE AS MANY SENTENCES AS YOU
CAN THAT START WITH:

I AM...

(THUMB PRINT)

I AM NOT...

(FEEL FREE TO DRAW ANYTHING AS YOU ARE INSPIRED)

I NOTICE...

I WONDER...

DESCRIBE THE EXPERIENCE OF RECEIVING THE BEST GIFT EVER:
(DRAW IT IF YOU CAN)

WHY WAS THIS GIFT IMPORTANT TO YOU?

DESCRIBE THE BEST EXPERIENCE OF GIVING A GIFT:
(DRAW IT IF YOU CAN)

WHY WAS THIS GIVING EXPERIENCE IMPORTANT TO YOU?

✔ IN WITH YOUR ACCOUNTABLE PERSON

(TAPE A STRAND OF YOUR HAIR HERE)

MEDITATE ON:

ARE NOT TWO SPARROWS SOLD FOR A PENNY? YET NOT ONE OF THEM WILL FALL TO THE GROUND OUTSIDE YOUR FATHER'S CARE. AND EVEN THE VERY HAIRS OF YOUR HEAD ARE ALL NUMBERED. SO DON'T BE AFRAID; YOU ARE WORTH MORE THAN MANY SPARROWS.

MATTHEW 10:29-31 NIV

COPY THIS SENTENCE AS MANY TIMES AS YOU NEED UNTIL YOU
BELIEVE IT: (USE ADDITIONAL PAPER IF NECESSARY)

I AM A BELOVED CHILD OF GOD, WITH WHOM GOD IS WELL PLEASED.
I AM A...

COLOR, MEDITATE, TAKE A PHOTO
AND POST IT #HOLYCURRENCIES

BELIEVE IT YET?
NO? KEEP GOING

NOW THAT YOU BELIEVE THIS, WHAT ARE YOU GOING
TO DO ABOUT IT?

BELOVED

LUKE 3:21-22

WEEK 6

GO EXERCISE:

CHOOSE ONE OR MORE:

REPORT YOUR EXPERIENCE:

PHYSICAL WELLNESS

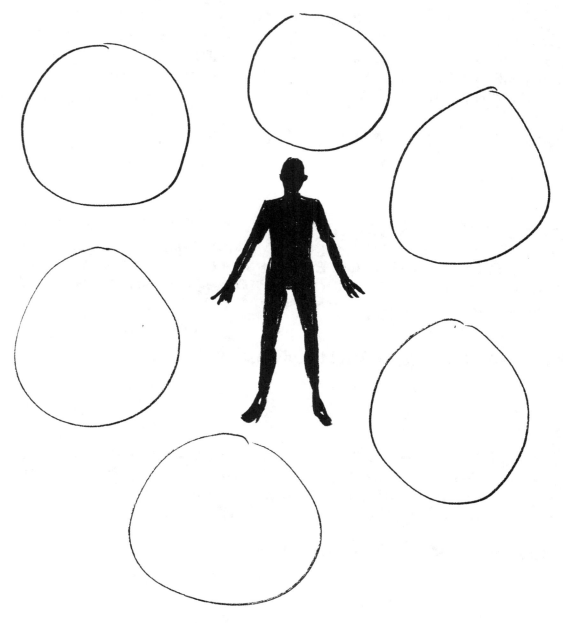

WRITE IN THE CIRCLES ABOVE, ELEMENTS THAT
CONTRIBUTE TO YOUR PHYSICAL WELLNESS.

STRENGTHS	WEAKNESSES	NEEDS	TO DO

WEEK 7

SIX DAYS YOU SHALL LABOR AND DO ALL YOUR WORK, BUT THE SEVENTH DAY IS A SABBATH TO THE LORD YOUR GOD. ON IT YOU SHALL NOT DO ANY WORK, NEITHER YOU, NOR YOUR SON OR DAUGHTER, NOR YOUR MALE OR FEMALE SERVANT, NOR YOUR OX, YOUR DONKEY OR ANY OF YOUR ANIMALS, NOR ANY FOREIGNER RESIDING IN YOUR TOWNS, SO THAT YOUR MALE AND FEMALE SERVANTS MAY REST, AS YOU DO.

DEUTERONOMY 5:13-14 (NIV)

I KNOW I AM PHYSICALLY WELL WHEN...

AT THE END OF EVERY SEVEN YEARS YOU MUST CANCEL DEBTS. THIS IS HOW IT IS TO BE DONE: EVERY CREDITOR SHALL CANCEL ANY LOAN THEY HAVE MADE TO A FELLOW ISRAELITE. THEY SHALL NOT REQUIRE PAYMENT FROM ANYONE AMONG THEIR OWN PEOPLE, BECAUSE THE LORD'S TIME FOR CANCELING DEBTS HAS BEEN PROCLAIMED.

DEUTERONOMY 15:1-2 (NIV)

I KNOW I AM ECONOMICALLY WELL WHEN...

FOR SIX YEARS YOU ARE TO SOW YOUR FIELDS AND HARVEST THE CROPS, BUT DURING THE SEVENTH YEAR LET THE LAND LIE UNPLOWED AND UNUSED. THEN THE POOR AMONG YOUR PEOPLE MAY GET FOOD FROM IT, AND THE WILD ANIMALS MAY EAT WHAT IS LEFT. EXODUS 23:10-11 (NIV

I KNOW THE EARTH IS WELL WHEN...

CONSECRATE THE FIFTIETH YEAR AND PROCLAIM LIBERTY THROUGHOUT THE LAND TO ALL ITS INHABITANTS. IT SHALL BE A JUBILEE FOR YOU; EACH OF YOU IS TO RETURN TO YOUR FAMILY PROPERTY AND TO YOUR OWN CLAN. THE FIFTIETH YEAR SHALL BE A JUBILEE FOR YOU; DO NOT SOW AND DO NOT REAP WHAT GROWS OF ITSELF OR HARVEST THE UNTENDED VINES. FOR IT IS A JUBILEE AND IT IS TO BE HOLY FOR YOU; EAT ONLY WHAT IS TAKEN DIRECTLY FROM THE FIELDS.

LEVITICUS 25:10-12 (NIV)

I KNOW I AM SPIRITUALLY WELL WHEN...

COLOR THIS PICTURE AS YOU MEDITATE ON THE TEXTS ON THE OPPOSITE PAGE. ✳ TAKE A PICTURE AND POST IT ONLINE. #HOLYCURRENCIES

WEEK 8

COMPLETE AS MANY SENTENCES AS YOU CAN:

I AM COMFORTABLE WHEN...

I DON'T HAVE TO CHANGE WHEN...

I DON'T HAVE TO LEARN NEW THINGS WHEN...

I FEEL SAFE WHEN...

I FEEL SECURE WHEN...

I AM COMPLACENT WHEN...

I FEEL SHELTERED WHEN...

I AM WILLING TO LEARN NEW THINGS WHEN...

I WILL EXPLORE THE POSSIBILITY OF CHANGE WHEN...

I WILL WANT TO DISCOVER NEW THINGS/WAYS WHEN...

I WILL DELVE INTO SOMETHING NEW WHEN...

I AM OPEN TO NEW IDEAS WHEN...

I WILL INVESTIGATE SOMETHING UNFAMILIAR WHEN...

I AM CURIOUS WHEN...

I AM WILLING TO STEP OUTSIDE OF MY BOUNDRY WHEN...

I AM ABLE TO BREAK THE BARRIERS THAT LIMIT ME WHEN...

I AM ABLE TO STEP OUT INTO THE MARGIN WHEN...

HAVE YOU ✓'D IN WITH YOUR ACCOUNTABLE PERSON?

PHILIPPIANS 4:12-13

MEDITATE ON PHILIPPIANS 4:12-13 (NRSV)

I KNOW WHAT IT IS TO HAVE LITTLE, AND I KNOW WHAT IT IS TO HAVE PLENTY. IN ANY AND ALL CIRCUMSTANCES I HAVE LEARNED THE SECRET OF BEING WELL-FED AND OF GOING HUNGRY, OF HAVING PLENTY AND OF BEING IN NEED. I CAN DO ALL THINGS THROUGH [CHRIST] WHO STRENGTHENS ME.

COMPLETE THE COMIC WITH YOUR DRAWING. WHAT SHOULD HAPPEN NEXT? (OR YOU CAN WRITE IT.)

COLOR, TAKE A PHOTO, AND POST #HOLYCURRENCIES

COMPLETE AS MANY SENTENCE AS YOU CAN:

WHEN I AM ANXIOUS, I...

WHEN I AM AFRAID, I...

WHEN I AM FEARFUL, I...

WHEN I AM SCARED, I...

WHEN I AM TROUBLED, I...

WHEN I NOTICE ANOTHER IS ANXIOUS, I...

WHEN I NOTICE ANOTHER IS AFRAID, I...

WHEN I NOTICE ANOTHER IS FEARFUL, I...

WHEN I NOTICE ANOTHER IS SCARED, I...

WHEN I NOTICE ANOTHER IS TROUBLED, I...

WHEN I _____, I WILL NOT BE ANXIOUS.

WHEN I _____, I WILL NOT BE AFRAID.

WHEN I _____, I WILL NOT BE FEARFUL.

WHEN I _____, I WILL NOT BE SCARED.

WHEN I _____, I WILL NOT BE TROUBLED.

WHEN WE _____, WE WILL NOT BE ANXIOUS.

WHEN WE _____, WE WILL NOT BE AFRAID.

WHEN WE _____, WE WILL NOT BE FEARFUL.

WHEN WE _____, WE WILL NOT BE SCARED.

WHEN WE _____, WE WILL NOT BE TROUBLED.

WEEK 11
EXCLUSIVE COMMUNITY

IN WHAT WAYS DOES A
COMMUNITY EXCLUDE
OTHERS WHO ARE NOT
LIKE THE PEOPLE
INSIDE?

WHAT ARE THEIR FEARS?

WHAT ARE THEY PROTECTING?

INCLUSIVE COMMUNITY

GRACE
MARGIN

WHAT WILL YOU DO TO
ASSIST A COMMUNITY
TO BECOME MORE
INCLUSIVE?

HOW CAN YOU MAKE ROOM
BETWEEN THE FEAR ZONE
AND THE SAFE ZONE?

HOW DO YOU INVITE PEOPLE
FROM THE INSIDE TO COME
OUT AND EXPLORE?

HOW DO YOU INVITE PEOPLE
FROM THE OUTSIDE TO
COME IN AND EXPLORE?

WRITE AN INVITATION USING THE FORMULA BELOW TO INVITE
A PERSON OR A GROUP TO COME TO A GRACIOUS INCLUSIVE
GATHERING. TRY THIS WITH YOUR FRIENDS WHO ARE ALSO
WORKING ON THIS BOOK.

· NAME THE FEARS THAT THE INVITEES WOULD HAVE.

· CREATE SENTENCES TO ADDRESS THEIR FEARS
BEGINNING WITH: WE WILL NOT...

· NAME THE PURPOSE AND PROCESS OF THE GATHERING.

· CREATE SENTENCES TO DESCRIBE THE PURPOSE AND
PROCESS: WE WILL...

FOLD ME

YOU'RE INVITED
TO COME TO:

_____

ON: _____
AT: _____

AT THIS GATHERING,
    WE WILL ...

    WE WILL NOT ...

    WE WILL ...

    WE WILL NOT ...

    I WANT TO DO THIS BECAUSE ...

IN ORDER FOR ANY COMMUNITY (FAMILY, CHURCH, WORKPLACE, SCHOOL, NEIGHBOR-HOOD, ETC.) TO BE SOCIALLY WELL, WE NEED TO CREATE AND AGREE ON A SET OF GROUND RULES FOR INTER-ACTION - COVENANT.

GO TO WWW.HOLYCURRENCIES.COM AND LISTEN TO THE SONG "OPEN SPACE" BY ERIC H.F. LAW

SELECT A COMMUNITY OF WHICH YOU ARE A PART. INTERVIEW AT LEAST 5 PEOPLE AND ASK THEM TO COMPLETE THE FOLLOWING SENTENCES. RECORD THEM IN THE SPACE PROVIDED:

COMMUNITY:

I KNOW I'M RESPECTED WHEN...	I KNOW I'M INCLUDED WHEN...	I KNOW I'M SUPPORTED WHEN...

REVIEW WHAT YOU HAVE COLLECTED. WHAT WOULD A COVENANT INCLUDE IF WE ARE TO FOSTER WELLNESS IN THIS COMMUNITY?

✔ TIME TO LET YOUR A.P. KNOW HOW YOU'RE DOING.

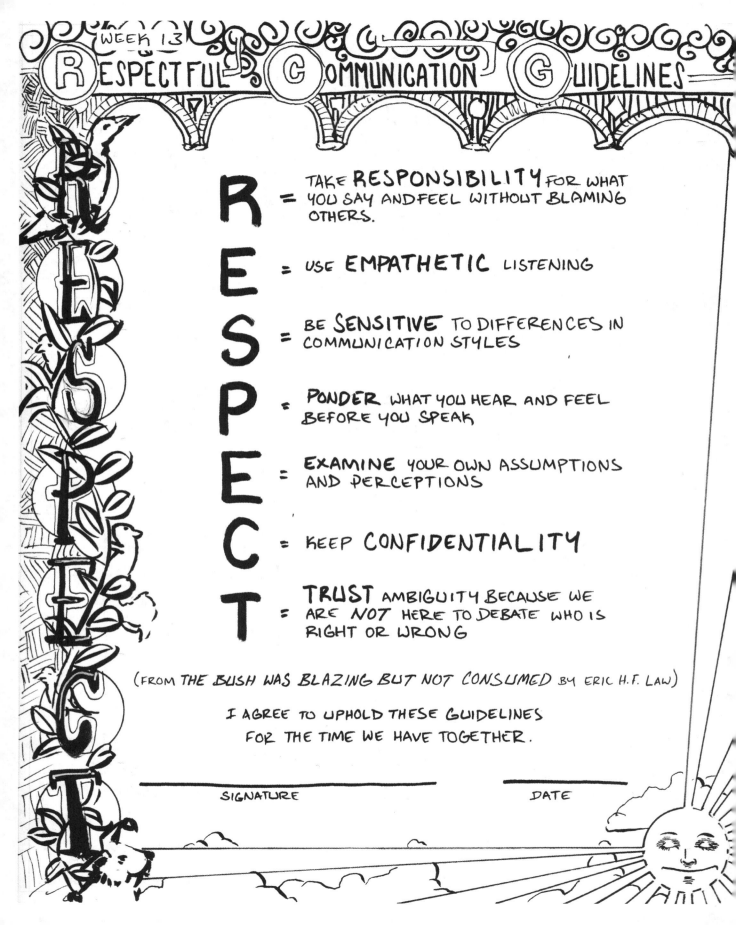

RESPECTFUL COMMUNICATION GUIDELINES

R = TAKE **RESPONSIBILITY** FOR WHAT YOU SAY AND FEEL WITHOUT BLAMING OTHERS.

E = USE **EMPATHETIC** LISTENING

S = BE **SENSITIVE** TO DIFFERENCES IN COMMUNICATION STYLES

P = **PONDER** WHAT YOU HEAR AND FEEL BEFORE YOU SPEAK

E = **EXAMINE** YOUR OWN ASSUMPTIONS AND PERCEPTIONS

C = KEEP **CONFIDENTIALITY**

T = **TRUST** AMBIGUITY BECAUSE WE ARE *NOT* HERE TO DEBATE WHO IS RIGHT OR WRONG

(FROM *THE BUSH WAS BLAZING BUT NOT CONSUMED* BY ERIC H.F. LAW)

I AGREE TO UPHOLD THESE GUIDELINES FOR THE TIME WE HAVE TOGETHER.

_____   _____
SIGNATURE   DATE

WATCH A VIDEO ON PRESENTING RCG
(WWW.HOLYCURRENCIES.COM)

FOLD ME

MEDITATE ON EACH ONE OF THE RESPECTFUL COMMUNICATION GUIDELINES.

WRITE DOWN YOUR THOUGHTS ON WHY THESE GUIDELINES ARE IMPORTANT AND WHAT YOU WOULD DO TO UPHOLD THEM (I HAVE PUT IN SOME OF MY THOUGHTS TO GET YOU STARTED ☺):

R.C.G.	WHY IS THIS GUIDELINE IMPORTANT?	WHAT WOULD I DO TO UPHOLD THIS GUIDELINE?
TAKE RESPONSIBILITY	BLAMING CAN SHUT DOWN COMMUNICATION.	USE "I" STATEMENTS
EMPATHETIC LISTENING	BUILD RELATIONSHIP	
SENSITIVE TO DIFFERENCES		
PONDER		
EXAMINE		
CONFIDENTIALITY		
TRUST AMBIGUITY	-SO WE CAN HEAR FROM EVERYONE. -SEE BETTER TRUTH TOGETHER	DON'T DEBATE. BE CURIOUS

NEXT TIME YOU GATHER A SMALL GROUP FOR SHARING AND DISCUSSION, TAKE 5 TO 10 MINUTES TO PRESENT THESE GUIDELINES AND INVITE THE GROUP TO AGREE TO UPHOLD THEM BEFORE YOU START THE CONVERSATIONS.

MATTHEW 20:16

1. BRING A GROUP OF PEOPLE TOGETHER.

2. SELECT TOPICS FOR SHARING. FOR EXAMPLE:
   - NAME
   - I HAVE BEEN LIVING IN THE COMMUNITY FOR _____
   - ONE THING I'M GOOD AT IS...
   - ONE THING I LOVE ABOUT THIS COMMUNITY IS...
   - ONE CONCERN I HAVE ABOUT OUR COMMUNITY IS...

3. INVITE EACH PERSON TO PONDER AND WRITE DOWN HIS/HER RESPONSE TO THESE TOPICS

4. DESCRIBE THE MUTUAL INVITATION PROCESS:

   > IN ORDER TO ENSURE THAT EVERYONE WHO WANTS TO SHARE **HAS** THE OPPORTUNITY TO SPEAK, WE WILL USE A PROCESS CALLED **MUTUAL INVITATION**:

   > I WILL SHARE FIRST. AFTER I HAVE SPOKEN, I THEN INVITE ANOTHER TO SHARE. AFTER THE NEXT PERSON HAS SPOKEN, THAT PERSON IS GIVEN THE PRIVILEGE TO INVITE ANOTHER TO SHARE. TRY NOT TO INVITE THE PERSON NEXT TO YOU SO THAT WE WON'T MOVE INTO THE HABIT OF GOING AROUND IN A CIRCLE.

   > IF YOU'RE NOT READY TO SHARE, SAY "I PASS FOR NOW," AND WE WILL INVITE YOU TO SHARE LATER ON. IF YOU DON'T WANT TO SAY ANYTHING AT ALL, SIMPLY SAY "PASS" AND PROCEED TO INVITE ANOTHER TO SHARE. WE WILL DO THIS UNTIL EVERYONE HAS BEEN INVITED.

   > I INVITE YOU TO LISTEN AND NOT TO RESPOND TO SOMEONE'S SHARING IMMEDIATELY. THERE WILL BE TIME TO RESPOND AND TO ASK CLARIFYING QUESTIONS AFTER EVERYONE HAS SHARED.

5. START THE INVITATION PROCESS AND INVITE EACH PERSON TO SHARE.

I NOTICE...   I WONDER...   WATCH A DEMONSTRATION VIDEO OF THIS PROCESS ON HOLYCURRENCIES.COM

FOLD ME

WEEK 15

BANG
BANG
BANG

LIST THE TOOLS AND SKILLS YOU HAVE:

WHAT ARE THE BLESSINGS THAT THESE TOOLS PROVIDE? FOR WHOM?

HOW WOULD YOU PASS THESE TOOLS AND SKILLS ON?
TO WHOM?

WEEK 16

LIST THE KNOWLEDGE AND ABILITIES THAT YOU HAVE:
(THIS CAN BE ANYTHING THAT YOU ARE GOOD AT.)

NAME SOME OF THE MINISTRIES IN YOUR CHURCH THAT COULD BENEFIT FROM YOUR ABILITIES:

NAME A PERSON OR A GROUP IN CHURCH WHO MIGHT BENEFIT FROM LEARNING THE SKILLS THAT YOU HAVE:

NAME A PERSON OR GROUP OUTSIDE OF CHURCH WHO MIGHT BENEFIT FROM LEARNING THE SKILLS THAT YOU HAVE:

WHAT ADDITIONAL LEADERSHIP SKILLS (ESPECIALLY GRACIOUS LEADERSHIP SKILLS) WOULD YOU LIKE TO ACQUIRE?

DO SOME RESEARCH TO FIND OUT WHAT LEADERSHIP TRAINING PROGRAMS IN YOUR AREA OF INTEREST ARE AVAILABLE THROUGH YOUR CHURCH OR IN THE COMMUNITY.

✔ TO SEE IF YOUR A.P. KNOWS WHAT YOU'VE DONE.

COMPLETE THE PLEDGE CARD ON THIS PAGE. FIND AN ACCOUNTABLE PERSON TO SIGN IT. TAKE A PHOTO AND SEND IT TO SOMEONE WHO OVERSEES STEWARDSHIP MINISTRY IN YOUR CHURCH.

LEADERSHIP

- I COMMIT TO OFFERING MY ABILITY TO _____ (NAME OF LEADERSHIP SKILLS) IN SUPPORT OF _____ (NAME OF EXISTING OR NEW MINISTRY IN MY CHURCH OR COMMUNITY).

- I COMMIT TO PARTICIPATING IN _____ (NAME OF LEADERSHIP TRAINING PROGRAMS) IN ORDER TO BECOME A MORE GRACIOUS LEADER* IN CHURCH AND/OR THE COMMUNITY.

- I COMMIT TO MENTORING AND/OR TRAINING _____ NEW LEADERS IN MY CHURCH TO DO/BE _____

- I COMMIT TO MENTORING AND/OR TRAINING _____ LEADERS IN THE COMMUNITY TO DO / BE _____

MY NAME: _____

_____
SIGNATURE

MY ACCOUNTABLE PERSON _____

_____
SIGNATURE

HOLY CURRENCY

I WILL GET THIS DONE BY _____

* LEADERSHIP IS ANYTHING YOU KNOW HOW TO DO THAT YOU ARE WILLING TO SHARE WITH OTHERS.

WEEK 17

ECCLESIASTES 3:1-8   OR LISTEN TO "TURN, TURN, TURN" BY THE BYRDS

FOR THIS WEEK, WRITE IN THE CALENDAR ON THE NEXT PAGE
HOW YOU SPEND YOUR TIME HOUR BY HOUR.

AT THE END OF THE WEEK, TABULATE HOW MUCH TIME
YOU SPENT ON EACH OF THE FOLLOWING CURRENCIES:

___ PLACE

___ GRACIOUS LEADERSHIP

___ RELATIONSHIP

___ TRUTH

___ WELLNESS

___ MONEY

WRITE WHAT YOU LEARNED HERE:

STRENGTHS   WEAKNESSES   CHALLENGES

HOW WOULD YOU CHANGE YOUR USE OF TIME NEXT WEEK?

	SUN	MON	TUES	WED	THURS	FRI	SAT
5							
6							
7							
8							
9							
10							
11							
12							
1							
2							
3							
4							
5							
6							
7							
8							
9							
10							
11							

LIST THE TALENTS AND SKILLS THAT YOU HAVE AND THAT YOU WOULD LOVE TO SHARE:

LIST SOME OF THE THINGS YOU AND YOUR FAMILY NEED HELP WITH IN YOUR DAILY LIFE:

SEARCH AND READ ABOUT THE "TIME BANK" CONCEPT.
IF IT INSPIRES YOU, DO SOME MORE RESEARCH ON THE IDEA.

GATHER SOME OF YOUR FRIENDS AND SHARE WITH THEM
VIDEOS AND OTHER PROCESSES THAT YOU DISCOVERED ON
HOW TO START A TIME BANK.

JUAN FIXES
MING'S
BICYCLE

IVELISSE
TUTORS
JUAN'S
DAUGHTER

MING
GIVES KALIFA
GUITAR
LESSONS

HAILE HELPS
IVELISSE MOVE

KALIFA
WALKS HAILE'S
DOGS

HOW IT WORKS:
• 1 HOUR OF WORK IS
EQUAL TO ONE TIME
CURRENCY DOLLAR.

• EARN AND SPEND
THEM WITH ANYONE
PARTICIPATING IN
YOUR TIME BANK.

NAME AN EXISTING OR NEW MINISTRY IN YOUR CHURCH THAT YOU ARE REALLY EXCITED ABOUT:

HOW MUCH TIME PER WEEK ARE YOU WILLING TO OFFER TO SUPPORT THIS MINISTRY?

NAME AN EXISTING OR NEW MINISTRY OUT IN THE COMMUNITY THAT YOU ARE REALLY EXCITED ABOUT:

HOW MUCH TIME PER WEEK ARE YOU WILLING TO OFFER TO SUPPORT THIS MINISTRY?

NAME AN EXISTING OR NEW MINISTRY THAT LENDS ITSELF TO THE SUPPORT OF NON-CHURCH MEMBERS:

USING YOUR NETWORK OF RELATIONSHIPS, HOW CAN YOU HELP GET OUTSIDE VOLUNTEERS TO OFFER THEIR TIME FOR THIS MINISTRY?

COMPLETE THE PLEDGE CARD ON THIS PAGE. FIND AN ACCOUNTABLE PERSON TO SIGN IT. TAKE A PHOTO AND SEND IT TO SOMEONE WHO OVERSEES STEWARDSHIP MINISTRY IN YOUR CHURCH.

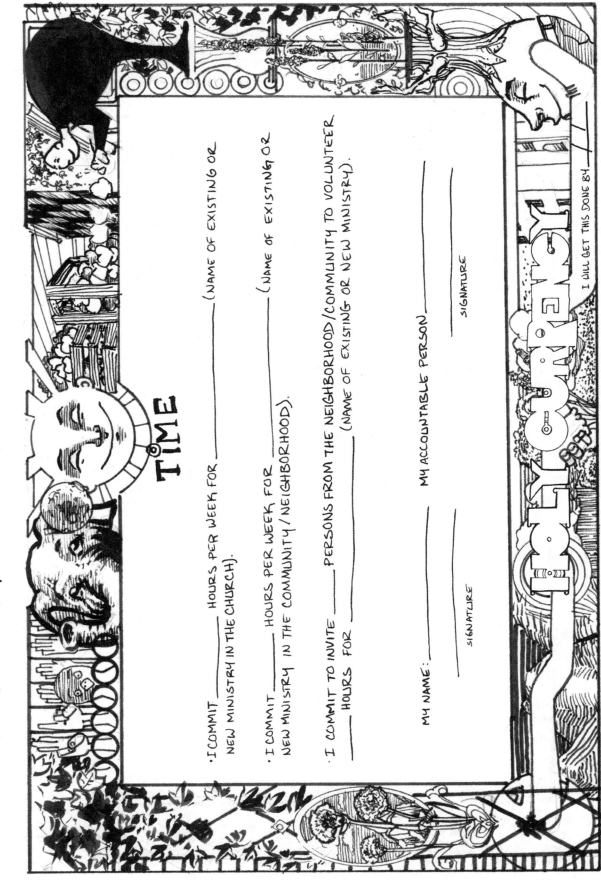

HOLY CURRENCY

TIME

• I COMMIT _____ HOURS PER WEEK FOR _____ (NAME OF EXISTING OR NEW MINISTRY IN THE CHURCH).

• I COMMIT _____ HOURS PER WEEK FOR _____ (NAME OF EXISTING OR NEW MINISTRY IN THE COMMUNITY/NEIGHBORHOOD).

• I COMMIT TO INVITE _____ PERSONS FROM THE NEIGHBORHOOD/COMMUNITY TO VOLUNTEER _____ HOURS FOR _____ (NAME OF EXISTING OR NEW MINISTRY).

MY NAME: _____

SIGNATURE

MY ACCOUNTABLE PERSON _____

SIGNATURE

I WILL GET THIS DONE BY _____

NAME A PERSON IN YOUR CHURCH WHOM YOU FEEL BLESSED TO KNOW

IN THIS RELATIONSHIP,

I RECEIVE...

I GIVE...

(TAPE, OR DRAW, A PICTURE OF
YOU AND YOUR FRIEND HERE)

WRITE A THANK-YOU NOTE TO THIS PERSON.

FIND A CREATIVE WAY TO DELIVER THIS THANK-YOU NOTE SO
YOU CAN DEEPEN THIS RELATIONSHIP.

NAME A PERSON OUTSIDE YOUR CHURCH WHOM YOU FEEL BLESSED TO KNOW

IN THIS RELATIONSHIP,

I RECEIVE...

I GIVE...

(TAPE, OR DRAW, A PICTURE OF
YOU AND YOUR FRIEND HERE)

WRITE A THANK-YOU NOTE TO THIS PERSON.

FIND A CREATIVE WAY TO DELIVER THIS THANK-YOU NOTE SO
YOU CAN DEEPEN THIS RELATIONSHIP.

✔ IN. DOES YOUR A.P. KNOW ABOUT YOUR RENEWED FRIENDSHIP?

WEEK 21

READ LUKE 10:38-42

I'M BEING A "MARTHA" WHEN...

I'M BEING A "MARY" WHEN...

DEVELOPING YOUR CURRENCY OF RELATIONSHIP

CREATE OPPORTUNITIES FOR FORMAL AND/OR INFORMAL CONVERSATIONS.

FOLD ME

START OR STRENGTHEN A RELATIONSHIP BY **PAYING ATTENTION** TO THE PERSON

HELP THE PERSON CLARIFY HIS/HER SELF-INTEREST BY **ASKING CLARIFYING QUESTIONS**

BE CURIOUS AND DISCOVER THE PERSON'S SELF-INTEREST BY LISTENING WITHOUT JUDGMENT.

WHAT'S A CLARIFYING QUESTION?

IT COMES FROM GENUINE CURIOSITY.

IT SEEKS INFORMATION AND UNDERSTANDING.

IT RESERVES JUDGMENT.

LET THE PERSON KNOW YOU HAVE BEEN LISTENING BY GIVING **FEEDBACK.**

TRY THIS PROCESS WITH SOMEONE YOU KNOW FOR 10 MINUTES. REPORT YOUR EXPERIENCE HERE:

ON THE NEXT PAGE WRITE "ME" IN THE CENTER SPOT, THEN WRITE IN THE NAMES OF 5 FRIENDS SURROUNDING YOU.

GO TO EACH FRIEND AND ASK THEM TO NAME 3 OF HIS/HER FRIENDS WHOM YOU DO NOT KNOW. WRITE THEM IN THE SPACES AROUND YOUR FRIEND.

ASK YOUR FRIEND TO SHARE SOMETHING IMPORTANT ABOUT EACH OF HIS/HER FRIENDS.

REPORT YOUR FINDINGS HERE:

I NOTICE...

I WONDER...

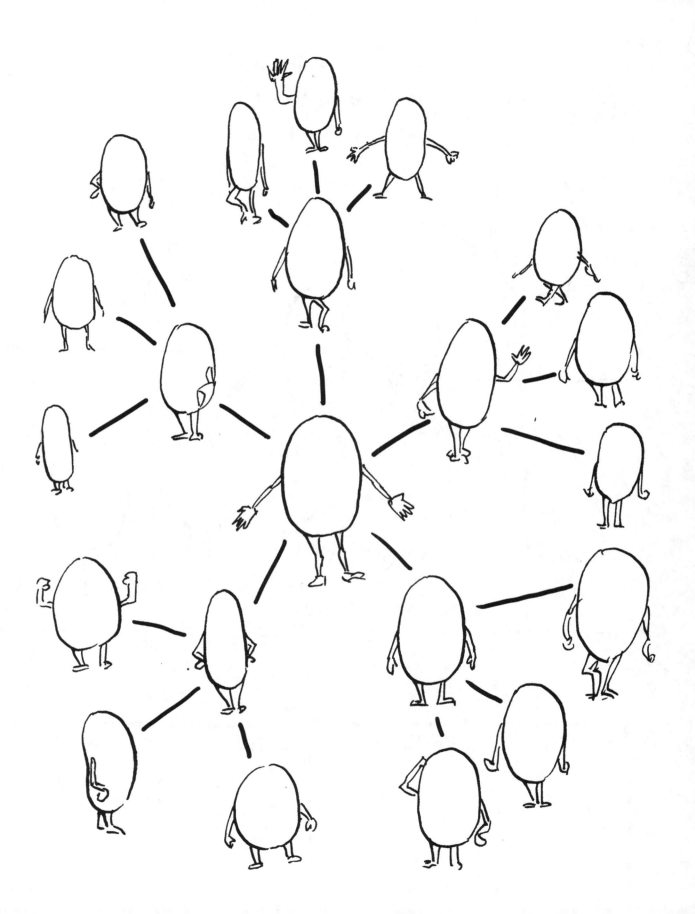

SOCIAL WELLNESS

DRAW OR WRITE THE NAMES OF THE PEOPLE OR GROUPS THAT CONTRIBUTE TO YOUR SOCIAL WELLNESS.

STRENGTHS:	WEAKNESSES:	NEEDS:	TO DO:

NAME THE PERSON(S) OR GROUP IN YOUR SOCIAL NETWORK WITH WHOM YOU WANT TO STRENGTHEN YOUR RELATIONSHIP THIS WEEK.

THE OPPORTUNITY I WILL CREATE FOR ME TO LISTEN TO THESE PEOPLE OR THIS GROUP IS:

(IF APPROPRIATE, INCORPORATE TIME TO PLAY AND/OR PRAY)

(TAPE, OR DRAW, A PICTURE OF YOU AND THESE PEOPLE HERE)

CONSIDER WRITING A GRACIOUS INVITATION (SEE WEEK 11)
REVIEW THE STEPS FOR DEVELOPING YOUR CURRENCY OF RELATIONSHIP.
(SEE WEEK 21)

NOW THAT YOU'VE DONE YOUR THING, REPORT YOUR EXPERIENCE BELOW:

BACKGROUND:	EXPERIENCES
INTERESTS	VALUES
PASSION	VISION/DREAM
CONCERNS	NEEDS

FOLD ME

LIST A FEW PEOPLE IN CHURCH YOU WANT TO GET TO KNOW BETTER:

LIST A FEW PEOPLE OUTSIDE YOUR CHURCH (IN THE WORKPLACE, SCHOOL, NEIGHBORHOOD, ETC.) WITH WHOM YOU WANT TO ESTABLISH A RELATIONSHIP:

LIST TWO PEOPLE YOU KNOW WHO MIGHT BENEFIT FROM GETTING TO KNOW EACH OTHER:

COMPLETE THE PLEDGE CARD ON THE NEXT PAGE. FIND AN ACCOUNTABLE PERSON TO SIGN IT. TAKE A PHOTO AND SEND IT TO SOMEONE WHO OVERSEES STEWARDSHIP MINISTRY IN YOUR CHURCH.

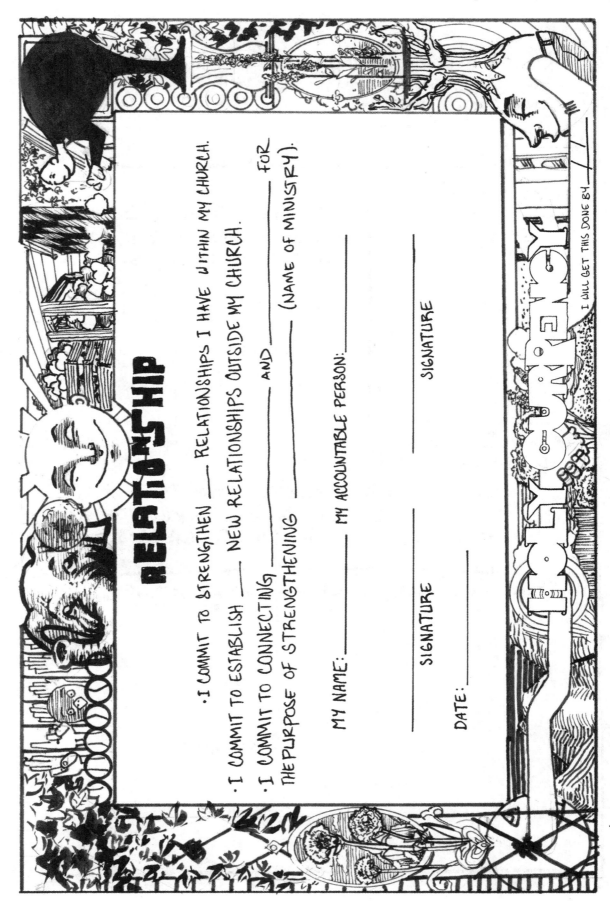

RELATIONSHIP

- I COMMIT TO STRENGTHEN _____ RELATIONSHIPS I HAVE WITHIN MY CHURCH.

- I COMMIT TO ESTABLISH _____ NEW RELATIONSHIPS OUTSIDE MY CHURCH.

- I COMMIT TO CONNECTING _____ AND _____ FOR
  THE PURPOSE OF STRENGTHENING _____ (NAME OF MINISTRY).

MY NAME: _____ MY ACCOUNTABLE PERSON: _____

SIGNATURE _____ SIGNATURE _____

DATE: _____

I WILL GET THIS DONE BY _____

✓ OUT WHAT YOUR A.P. THINKS ABOUT ALL THIS!

WEEK 25

NAME A PERSON IN YOUR CHURCH WHOM YOU WANT TO GET TO KNOW BECAUSE YOU THINK YOU MIGHT HAVE SIMILAR INTERESTS:

THE OPPORTUNITY I WILL CREATE FOR ME TO LISTEN TO THIS PERSON IS:

(TAPE, OR DRAW, A PICTURE OF YOU AND THESE PEOPLE HERE)

CONSIDER WRITING A GRACIOUS INVITATION (SEE WEEK 11)
REVIEW THE STEPS FOR DEVELOPING YOUR CURRENCY OF RELATIONSHIP
BEFORE MEETING WITH THIS PERSON (SEE WEEK 21).

NOW THAT YOU'VE DONE YOUR THING, REPORT YOUR EXPERIENCE BELOW:

BACKGROUND:	EXPERIENCES
INTERESTS	VALUES
PASSION	VISION/DREAM
CONCERNS	NEEDS

NAME A PERSON OUTSIDE YOUR CHURCH WHOM YOU WANT TO GET TO KNOW BECAUSE YOU THINK YOU MIGHT HAVE SIMILAR INTERESTS:

THE OPPORTUNITY I WILL CREATE FOR ME TO LISTEN TO THIS PERSON IS:

(TAPE, OR DRAW, A PICTURE OF YOU AND THESE PEOPLE HERE)

CONSIDER WRITING A GRACIOUS INVITATION.
(REVIEW THE STEPS FOR DEVELOPING YOUR CURRENCY OF RELATIONSHIP BEFORE MEETING WITH THIS PERSON)

NOW THAT YOU'VE DONE YOUR THING, REPORT YOUR EXPERIENCE BELOW:

BACKGROUND:	EXPERIENCES
INTERESTS	VALUES
PASSION	VISION/DREAM
CONCERNS	NEEDS

WEEK 26

NAME YOUR BEST FRIEND: _____

(DRAW OR GLUE A PICTURE OF
YOUR BEST FRIEND HERE)

WHAT IS IT ABOUT THIS PERSON THAT MAKES HIM/HER
YOUR BEST FRIEND?

WHAT DO YOU HAVE IN COMMON?

HOW ARE YOU DIFFERENT?

IN WHAT WAYS HAS THIS PERSON HELPED YOU BE "WELL"?

WRITE A THANK YOU NOTE AND DELIVER IT.
WRITE A GRACIOUS INVITATION (G.I.) TO INVITE THIS PERSON FOR A
GRACIOUS CONVERSATION WITH YOU (REVIEW HOW TO WRITE A G.I.
IN WEEK 11).

NAME SOMEONE WHOM YOU CONSIDER AS AN ENEMY

WHAT IS IT ABOUT THIS PERSON THAT MAKES HIM/HER YOUR ENEMY?

WHAT DO YOU HAVE IN COMMON?

(DRAW OR GLUE A PICTURE OF THIS ENEMY HERE)

HOW ARE YOU DIFFERENT?

IN WHAT WAYS HAS THIS PERSON BEEN NOT HELPFUL TO YOUR WELLNESS?

WRITE A LETTER TO THIS PERSON DESCRIBING YOUR EXPERIENCE AND IF APPROPRIATE, INCLUDE A GRACIOUS INVITATION TO INVITE THIS PERSON FOR A GRACIOUS CONVERSATION WITH YOU.

IMPORTANT: IF THIS PERSON IS PHYSICALLY AND EMOTIONALLY ABUSIVE, DO NOT DO THIS ALONE. THE INVITATION SHOULD INCLUDE THE PRESENCE OF ANOTHER TRUSTED PERSON WHO WILL SUPPORT YOU. THE LOCATION OF THE MEETING SHOULD BE A PUBLIC PLACE.

ALSO IMPORTANT: AT THE MEETING, INVITE THOSE PRESENT TO AGREE TO UPHOLD THE RESPECTFUL COMMUNICATION GUIDELINES. IF THERE IS NO AGREEMENT, WALK AWAY.

WEEK 27

OH GOD, PLEASE LET US DEFEAT THEM!

OH GOD, PLEASE LET US WIN!

BUT I LOVE THEM BOTH.

SCRATCH SCRATCH

YOU KNOW WHAT...?!

I DON'T CARE WHO WINS!

JUST PLAY AND HAVE FUN.

THEN MAYBE THROW A PARTY.

BUT I SAY TO YOU, LOVE YOUR ENEMIES AND PRAY FOR THOSE WHO PERSECUTE YOU, SO THAT YOU MAY BE CHILDREN OF YOUR FATHER IN HEAVEN; FOR HE MAKES HIS SUN RISE ON THE EVIL AND ON THE GOOD, AND SENDS RAIN ON THE RIGHTEOUS AND ON THE UNRIGHTEOUS.

(MATTHEW 5:44-45 NRSV)

THE DIALOGUE SONG

(FIND THIS SONG BY ERIC H.F. LAW AT WWW.HOLYCURRENCIES.COM AND LISTEN TO IT)

IF GOD LOVES ME
AND GOD LOVES YOU,
WHAT HAPPENS WHEN WE DISAGREE?
WHAT ARE WE GONNA DO?
WHAT ARE WE GONNA DO?

I NOTICE...

IF I LISTEN TO YOU
AND YOU LISTEN TO ME,
IN BETWEEN YOUR WORDS AND MINE,
WE MAY HEAR THE WORD OF GOD DIVINE.
IF YOU WALK WITH ME
AND I WALK WITH YOU,
IN BETWEEN MY WAY AND YOURS,
WE CAN FIND THE SACRED PATH
THAT LEADS TO MANY GRACIOUS OPEN DOORS

I WONDER...

IF I SEE WHAT YOU SEE
AND YOU SEE WHAT I SEE,
IN BETWEEN YOUR VIEW AND MINE,
WE MAY SEE THE VIEW OF GOD'S DESIGN.
IF YOU KNOW MY FEARS
AND I KNOW YOUR FEARS
IN BETWEEN MY FEARS AND YOURS,
WE CAN BUILD A PLACE THAT'S SAFE
WHERE JUSTICE REIGNS WITH GRACE AND NOT WITH WARS.

IF GOD LOVES ME
AND GOD LOVES YOU,
WHAT HAPPENS WHEN WE DISAGREE?
WHAT ARE WE GONNA DO?
WHAT ARE WE GONNA DO?

IMAGINE

IMAGINE A MILLIONAIRE AND A HOMELESS PERSON ARE BROTHERS; WHAT WOULD THEY BE TALKING ABOUT?

IMAGINE A POLICEMAN AND THE YOUNG MEN IN THE NEIGHBORHOOD ARE BROTHERS; WHAT WOULD THEY BE DOING IN THE NEIGHBORHOOD?

COLOR, TAKE A PHOTO, AND POST #HOLYCURRENCIES

IMAGINE REPUBLICAN AND DEMOCRATS ARE SISTERS AND BROTHERS; HOW WOULD THEY BEHAVE IN CONGRESS?

IMAGINE THE MARKETING DIRECTOR OF A DRUG COMPANY AND A PATIENT ARE SISTERS; HOW WOULD THE NEW DRUG BE PRICED AND ADVERTISED?

IMAGINE THE BANK LOAN OFFICER AND A POTENTIAL HOME BUYER ARE BROTHER AND SISTER; WHAT WOULD THE LOAN PROCESS BE LIKE?

SIT AT A LOCATION IN YOUR
NEIGHBORHOOD WHERE
THERE ARE PEOPLE AROUND,
WHOM YOU MAY OR MAY NOT KNOW.

...IT IS THAT VERY SPIRIT
BEARING WITNESS WITH
OUR SPIRIT THAT WE
ARE CHILDREN OF GOD,
AND IF CHILDREN, THEN
HEIRS, HEIRS OF GOD AND
JOINT HEIRS WITH CHRIST-
IF, IN FACT, WE SUFFER
WITH HIM SO THAT WE MAY
ALSO BE GLORIFIED
WITH HIM.
  -ROMANS 8:16-17 NRSV

SELECT ONE PERSON WHO IS VERY DIFFERENT FROM YOU.
WRITE OR DRAW A SCENARIO OR A DIALOGUE THAT YOU
WOULD HAVE WITH THE PERSON AS IF THIS PERSON WERE
YOUR BROTHER OR SISTER.

COLOR, TAKE A PHOTO, AND POST #HOLYCURRENCIES

✓OUT WHAT YOUR A.P. THINKS ABOUT ALL THIS!

AS YOU COLOR THE NEXT PAGE, MEDITATE ON:

> I AM THE WAY AND THE TRUTH AND THE LIFE. NO ONE
> COMES TO THE FATHER EXCEPT THROUGH ME.
> JOHN 14:6 NRSV

WHEN YOU GET TO COLORING IN THE WORD "TRUTH,"
CONSIDER THE HEBREW WORD THAT IS TRANSLATED
AS TRUTH, *EMET*, IS COMPOSED OF THE THREE
LETTERS, א - ALEF, מ - MEM, ת - TAV - THE FIRST,
MIDDLE, AND LAST LETTERS OF THE HEBREW
ALPHABET.

THEN MEDITATE ON WHY JESUS PUT THE WORD "TRUTH"
IN BETWEEN "WAY" AND "LIFE."

WRITE OR DRAW THE FRUIT OF YOUR MEDITATION HERE:

I NOTICE...   I WONDER...

COLOR, TAKE A PHOTO, AND POST #HOLYCURRENCIES

NAME A PERSONAL OR FAMILY ISSUE OF WHICH YOU WANT TO DISCERN THE TRUTH:

WHY IS THIS IMPORTANT?

NAME A CHURCH ISSUE OF WHICH YOU WANT TO DISCERN THE TRUTH:

WHY IS THIS IMPORTANT?

NAME A NEIGHBORHOOD COMMUNITY ISSUE OF WHICH YOU WANT TO DISCERN THE TRUTH:

WHY IS THIS IMPORTANT?

NAME AN ENVIRONMENTAL ISSUE OF WHICH YOU WANT DISCERN THE TRUTH:

WHY IS THIS IMPORTANT?

COMPLETE THE PLEDGE CARD ON THE NEXT PAGE. FIND AN ACCOUNTABLE PERSON TO SIGN IT. TAKE A PHOTO AND SEND IT TO SOMEONE WHO OVERSEES STEWARDSHIP MINISTRY IN YOUR CHURCH.

TRUTH

- I COMMIT TO DISCOVER/DISCERN THE TRUTH ABOUT _____ FOR MYSELF AND/OR MY FAMILY.

- I COMMIT TO DISCERN THE TRUTH ABOUT _____ IN MY CHURCH.

- I COMMIT TO DISCERN THE TRUTH ABOUT _____ IN MY NEIGHBORHOOD, MY TOWN/CITY OR MY COUNTRY.

- I COMMIT TO DISCERN THE TRUTH ABOUT _____ ABOUT THE EARTH.

MY NAME: _____ MY ACCOUNTABLE PERSON: _____

SIGNATURE _____ SIGNATURE _____

DATE: _____

HOLY CURRENCY

I WILL GET THIS DONE BY _____

COLOR, TAKE A PHOTO, AND POST #HOLYCURRENCIES

SELECT A COMMUNITY ISSUE OF WHICH YOU WOULD WANT TO LEARN THE TRUTH:

NAME THE POWERFUL PEOPLE AND THEIR PERSPECTIVES ON THE ISSUE:

NAME THE POWERLESS WHO ARE ON THE GROUND WORKING ON THIS ISSUE IN YOUR COMMUNITY:

DESCRIBE HOW YOU WOULD GET AT THE TRUTH BY LISTENING TO THE POWERLESS PEOPLE ON THIS ISSUE. CONSIDER USING THE GRACIOUS SKILLS: GRACIOUS INVITATION (WEEK 13), RESPECTFUL COMMUNICATION GUIDELINES (WEEK 13), AND MUTUAL INVITATION (WEEK 14):

GO AND LISTEN TO THE POWERLESS PEOPLE AS YOU HAVE PLANNED AND REPORT YOUR FINDINGS HERE:

I NOTICE...

I WONDER...

NAME A PERSON WHO IS VERY DIFFERENT FROM YOU IN YOUR CHURCH WHOM YOU WANT TO GET TO KNOW.

THE OPPORTUNITY I WILL CREATE FOR FOR ME TO LISTEN TO THIS PERSON IS:

CONSIDER WRITING A GRACIOUS INVITATION

(TAPE, OR DRAW, A PICTURE OF YOU AND THIS PERSON HERE)

(REVIEW THE STEPS FOR DEVELOPING YOUR CURRENCY OF RELATIONSHIP)

REPORT YOUR EXPERIENCE BELOW:

BACKGROUND:	EXPERIENCES
INTERESTS	VALUES
PASSION	VISION/DREAM
CONCERNS	NEEDS

NAME A PERSON WHO IS VERY DIFFERENT FROM YOU OUTSIDE YOUR CHURCH WHOM YOU WANT TO GET TO KNOW.

THE OPPORTUNITY I WILL CREATE FOR FOR ME TO LISTEN TO THIS PERSON IS:

CONSIDER WRITING A GRACIOUS INVITATION

(TAPE, OR DRAW, A PICTURE OF YOU AND THIS PERSON HERE)

(REVIEW THE STEPS FOR DEVELOPING YOUR CURRENCY OF RELATIONSHIP)

REPORT YOUR EXPERIENCE BELOW:

BACKGROUND:	EXPERIENCES
INTERESTS	VALUES
PASSION	VISION/DREAM
CONCERNS	NEEDS

✓IN WITH YOUR FAVORITE A.P.

WEEK 33

LUKE 6:20-26

COLOR, TAKE A PHOTO, AND POST #HOLYCURRENCIES

SELECT A COMMUNITY ISSUE ABOUT WHICH YOU WOULD WANT TO LEARN THE TRUTH:

NAME THE POWERFUL PEOPLE AND THEIR PERSPECTIVES ON THE ISSUE:

NAME THE POWERLESS PEOPLE IN YOUR COMMUNITY ON THIS ISSUE:

DESCRIBE HOW YOU WOULD GET AT THE TRUTH BY LISTENING TO THE POWERLESS PEOPLE ON THIS ISSUE:
CONSIDER USING THE GRACIOUS SKILLS: G.I. (WEEK 13), RCG (WEEK 13) AND M I (WEEK 14)

TALK TO THESE POWERLESS PEOPLE AND REPORT YOUR FINDINGS HERE:

I NOTICE...

I WONDER ...

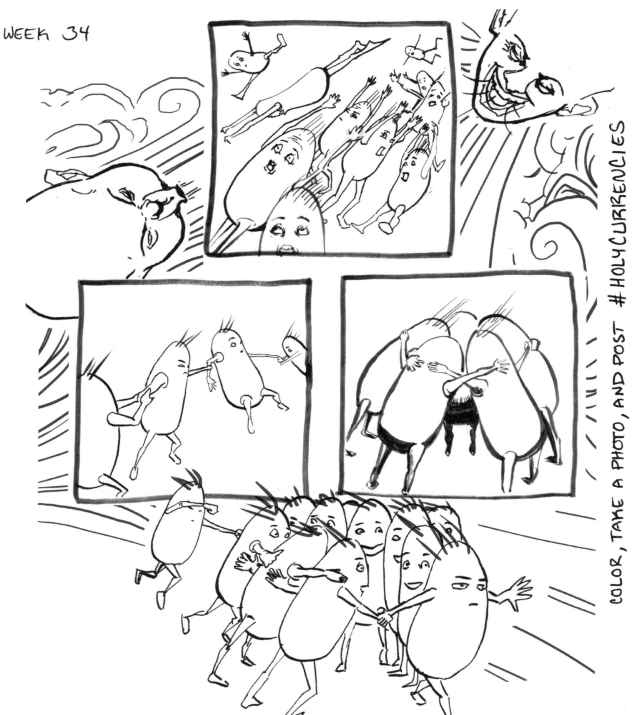

WE MUST NO LONGER BE CHILDREN, TOSSED TO AND FRO AND BLOWN ABOUT BY EVERY WIND OF DOCTRINE, BY PEOPLE'S TRICKERY, BY THEIR CRAFTINESS IN DECEITFUL SCHEMING. BUT SPEAKING THE TRUTH IN LOVE, WE MUST GROW UP IN EVERY WAY INTO HIM WHO IS THE HEAD, INTO CHRIST, FROM WHOM THE WHOLE BODY, JOINED AND KNIT TOGETHER BY EVERY LIGAMENT WITH WHICH IT IS EQUIPPED, AS EACH PART IS WORKING PROPERLY, PROMOTES THE BODY'S GROWTH IN BUILDING ITSELF UP IN LOVE.

EPHESIANS 4:14-16 (NRSV)

COLOR, TAKE A PHOTO, AND POST #HOLYCURRENCIES

NAME AN ISSUE THAT HAS PUZZLED OR CONFUSED YOU RECENTLY.

- WHAT ARE THE "WIND OF DOCTRINE" THAT HAVE TOSSED YOU AND YOUR FRIENDS TO AND FRO?

- WHO OR WHAT GROUPS WERE DOING THE "BLOWING"?

CREATE OPPORTUNITIES TO GET TOGETHER WITH YOUR FRIENDS. CONSIDER WRITING A GI., RCG AND MI.

- INVITE EACH PERSON TO "SPEAK THE TRUTH IN LOVE" ABOUT THEIR EXPERIENCES ON THIS ISSUE. (DON'T FORGET TO PRESENT RESPECTFUL COMMUNICATION GUIDELINE FIRST AND USE MUTUAL INVITATION FROM WEEKS 13 & 14)

- HAVING LISTENED TO EACH OTHER'S "TRUTH," DECIDE TOGETHER WHAT YOU ARE GOING TO DO TO ADDRESS THIS ISSUE TOGETHER.

WRITE OR DRAW YOUR PLAN HERE:

WEEK 35

DRAW THE FLOOR PLAN (INCLUDING OUTDOOR SPACES IF YOU HAVE
THEM) OF YOUR HOME HERE:

GO INTO EACH SPACE AND HAVE A QUIET TIME. DRAW OR WRITE IN
THE FLOOR PLAN HOW THIS SPACE HAS BEEN USED. THEN WRITE
DOWN THE TIME SPENT AND THE BLESSINGS YOU AND/OR
OTHERS RECEIVED IN THAT SPACE ON THE NEXT PAGE.

SPACE	TIME SPENT / WEEK	BLESSINGS RECEIVED
KITCHEN		
LIVING ROOM		
BEDROOM		
HALL		

I NOTICE...

 I WONDER...

WEEK 36

DRAW THE FLOOR PLAN (INCLUDING OUTDOOR SPACES) OF
YOUR CHURCH HERE:

GET TOGETHER WITH AT LEAST 3 CHURCH MEMBERS
AND GO INTO EACH SPACE AND HAVE A QUIET TIME.
DRAW OR WRITE IN THE FLOOR PLAN HOW THIS SPACE
HAS BEEN USED THROUGHOUT THE WEEK.

THEN WRITE DOWN THE TIME SPENT AND THE
BLESSINGS YOU AND/OR OTHERS RECEIVED
IN THAT SPACE IN THE NEXT PAGE.

✓IN WITH YOUR A.P.

SPACE	WHO SPENDS TIME HERE?	HOW MUCH TIME PER WEEK?	BLESSINGS RECEIVED
SANCTUARY			
PARKING LOT			

I NOTICE...

I WONDER...

COLOR, TAKE A PHOTO, AND POST #HOLYCURRENCIES

INVITE 2 TO 3 PEOPLE TO DO A WALKING TOUR OF YOUR NEIGHBORHOOD.

LOOK FOR SIGNS OF PHYSICAL, SOCIAL, ECONOMIC, SPIRITUAL AND ECOLOGICAL WELLNESS AND UNWELLNESS.

DESCRIBE THEM ON THE NEXT PAGE.

	SIGNS OF WELLNESS	SIGNS OF UNWELLNESS
PHYSICAL		
SOCIAL		
ECONOMIC		
SPIRITUAL		
ECOLOGICAL		

WEEK 38

DRAW PICTURES (OR YOU CAN WRITE) TO DESCRIBE
3 PLACES IN YOUR COMMUNITY THAT ARE DOING WELL
(PHYSICALLY, SOCIALLY, SPIRITUALLY, ECOLOGICALLY
AND ECONOMICALLY).

DO SOME RESEARCH THIS WEEK TO DISCOVER THE TRUTH
OF WHY AT LEAST ONE OF THESE PLACES IS DOING WELL.
(TRY A WEB SEARCH, LISTEN TO PEOPLE, LIBRARY, ETC.)

WRITE OR DRAW YOUR FINDINGS HERE:

IN WHAT WAYS CAN YOU AND/OR CHURCH COMMUNITY
PARTNER WITH THESE PLACES TO FOSTER EVEN
GREATER WELLNESS?

WEEK 39

DRAW PICTURES (OR YOU CAN WRITE) TO DESCRIBE
3 PLACES IN YOUR COMMUNITY THAT ARE NOT DOING
WELL (PHYSICALLY, SOCIALLY, SPIRITUALLY,
ECOLOGICALLY AND ECONOMICALLY).

DO SOME RESEARCH THIS WEEK TO DISCOVER THE TRUTH OF WHY AT LEAST ONE OF THE PLACES IS NOT DOING WELL. TRY GOOGLE, LISTENING TO PEOPLE, LIBRARY, ETC.

WRITE ABOUT OR DRAW YOUR FINDINGS HERE:

ARE THERE ANY CURRENCIES YOU CAN OFFER TO ASSIST IN MOVING THIS PLACE TOWARD GREATER WELLNESS?

WEEK 40

NAME A MINISTRY IN YOUR CHURCH THAT CAN BE ENHANCED BY HAVING A BETTER SPACE OR LOCATION WITHIN YOUR CHURCH'S PROPERTIES:

IN WHAT WAYS CAN YOU HELP TO RENOVATE, BEAUTIFY OR REFURBISH THIS PLACE?

IF YOU OWN OR RENT ANY PROPERTIES, LIST THEM HERE:

IN WHAT WAYS CAN YOU OFFER THE USE OF ONE OF THESE PROPERTIES FOR MINISTRY? WHICH MINISTRY WOULD BE A GOOD MATCH FOR THIS PLACE?

LIST SPACES YOU HAVE ACCESS TO (HOME, WORKPLACE, PUBLIC SPACES, ETC.):

IN WHAT WAYS CAN YOU MAKE ONE OF THESE PLACES AVAILABLE FOR MINISTRIES? WHICH MINISTRY WOULD BE A GOOD MATCH FOR THIS PLACE?

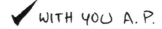 WITH YOU A.P.

COMPLETE THE PLEDGE CARD ON THIS PAGE. FIND AN ACCOUNTABLE PERSON TO SIGN IT. TAKE A PHOTO AND SEND IT TO SOMEONE WHO OVERSEES STEWARDSHIP MINISTRY IN YOUR CHURCH.

PLACE

· I COMMIT TO RENOVATE / BEAUTIFY / REFURBISH _____ (LOCATION OF CHURCH PROPERTY) FOR _____ (NAME OF EXISTING OR NEW MINISTRY).

· I COMMIT _____ (LOCATION I OWN) FOR _____ (NAME OF EXISTING OR NEW MINISTRY); AND

· I COMMIT TO MAKING _____ (LOCATION TO WHICH I HAVE ACCESS) AVAILABLE FOR _____ (NAME OF EXISTING OR NEW MINISTRY).

MY NAME: _____

_____
SIGNATURE

MY ACCOUNTABLE PERSON

_____
SIGNATURE

PLAY CURRENCY

I WILL GET THIS DONE BY _____

SPIRITUAL WELLNESS

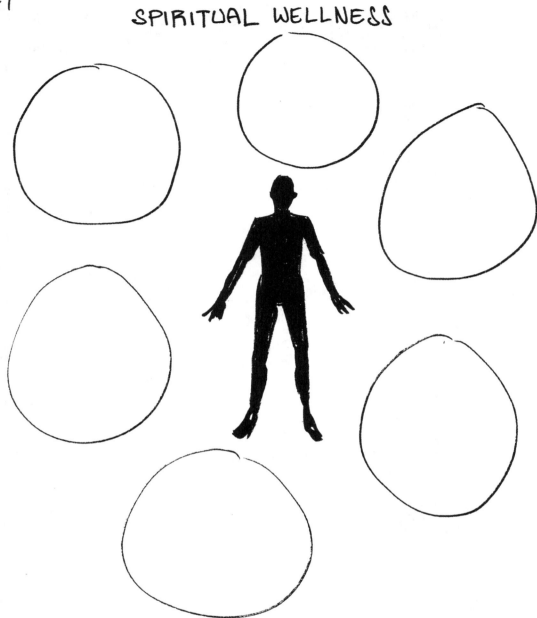

WRITE IN THE CIRCLES ABOVE PEOPLE, GROUPS, AND PLACES THAT CONTRIBUTE TO YOUR SPIRITUAL WELLNESS.

STRENGTHS	WEAKNESSES	NEEDS	TO DO

COMPLETE THESE
SENTENCES AS YOU BREATHE...

I BREATHE IN...

I BREATHE OUT...

I BREATHE IN...

I BREATHE OUT...

I BREATHE IN...

I BREATHE OUT...

I BREATHE IN...

I BREATHE OUT...

I BREATHE IN...

I BREATHE OUT...

I BREATHE IN...

I BREATHE OUT...

I NOTICE...   I WONDER...

COLOR, TAKE A PHOTO, AND POST #HOLYCURRENCIES

WHAT IF YOUR WORTH IS DETERMINED BY HOW MUCH YOU GIVE AWAY?

THINGS TO GIVE AWAY	TO WHOM	BLESSING EXCHANGE
_____	_____	_____
_____	_____	_____
_____	_____	_____
_____	_____	_____
_____	_____	_____
_____	_____	_____

I NOTICE . . .

I WONDER . . . .

$60,000,000

WHO WANTS TO SPEND $60,000,000 FOR A POLITICAL CAMPAIGN?

A. PAY A YEAR OF MORTGAGE PAYMENTS FOR 10,000 FAMILIES.

B. PAY A YEAR OF HEALTH INSURANCE FOR 10,000 FAMILIES.

C. CREATE 6,000 VOTER EDUCATION PROGRAMS.

D. CREATE 1,000 JOBS WITH GOOD BENEFITS

E. CREATE A VENTURE CAPITAL FUND TO START 200 NEW BUSINESSES.

F. BUY NASTY ATTACK ADS AGAINST MY OPPONENTS.

COLOR, TAKE A PHOTO, AND POST #HOLYCURRENCIES

RECALL AN EARLIER TIME IN YOUR LIFE WHEN MONEY WAS USED IN A WAY THAT GAVE BLESSINGS.

DRAW OR WRITE THE STORY OF WHAT HAPPENED HERE. CONSIDER WHERE YOU WERE, WHERE THE MONEY CAME FROM, WHO BENEFITED FROM THIS, AND WHAT BLESSINGS WERE EXCHANGED.

HOW DID THIS EXPERIENCE IMPACT THE WAY YOU USE MONEY TODAY?

WEEK 44

HOLD A BILL (IT CAN BE #1, #5, #20, OR #100) IN YOUR HAND.
EXAMINE IT CLOSELY (FRONT AND BACK), THE GRAPHICS,
THE WORDS, THE NUMBERS, ETC. THEN TAPE IT IN THE
FRAME BELOW.

(TAPE BILL HERE)

I NOTICE _____

I WONDER _____

I CAN EXCHANGE THIS BILL FOR:

THE BLESSINGS THAT MAY COME FROM THIS EXCHANGE:

_____ → _____

_____ → _____

_____ → _____

_____ → _____

_____ → _____

_____ → _____

CHOOSE THE BLESSING YOU WANT TO PROVIDE AND DESCRIBE HOW YOU WOULD SPEND THIS MONEY:

SHARE THIS IDEA WITH YOUR FRIENDS WHO ARE DOING THIS EXERCISE. ARE THERE POSSIBILITIES OF JOINING FORCES TO INCREASE THE BLESSINGS EXCHANGE?

✓ HOW'S YOUR A.P. DOING?

ASK EVERYONE IN YOUR HOUSEHOLD TO SAVE AND PRINT
OUT ALL THE RECEIPTS FOR EVERYTHING THEY PAID
FOR DURING THE WEEK.

(CLIP RECEIPTS HERE)

AT THE END OF THE WEEK, TABULATE THE RECEIPTS:

FOOD	$ _____
TRANSPORTATION	$ _____
ENTERTAINMENT	$ _____
MEDICAL	$ _____
SUPPLIES	$ _____
OTHERS	$ _____

THE MINIMUM WAGE IN MY STATE IS $ _____

GATHER THE PEOPLE IN YOUR HOUSEHOLD
AND DISCUSS:

WHAT WOULD BE YOUR TOTAL HOUSEHOLD INCOME PER WEEK IF
EVERYONE WHO IS WORKING ONLY MADE MINIMUM WAGE?

HOUSEHOLD WEEKLY MINIMUM WAGE INCOME: _____ PER WEEK

SUBTRACT 30% OF THE INCOME AS RENT OF YOUR HOME. THE
TOTAL BUDGET FOR THE WEEK IS: _____ PER WEEK.

IF EVERYONE IN YOUR HOUSEHOLD WERE TO LIVE ON THIS BUDGET
FOR A WEEK, WHAT WOULD YOU KEEP AND WHAT WOULD YOU
CUT?

NEW MINIMUM WAGE BUDGET

FOOD $ _____
TRANSPORTATION $ _____
ENTERTAINMENT $ _____
MEDICAL $ _____
SUPPLIES $ _____
OTHERS $ _____

TRY LIVING ON THIS BUDGET THIS COMING WEEK.
DONATE THE MONEY YOU SAVE TO A CHARITY.

WEEK 46

WRITE DOWN ALL THE THINGS YOU CAN DO WITH 10% OF YOUR INCOME THIS WEEK THAT WILL GIVE BLESSINGS TO OTHERS.

10% OF THIS WEEK'S INCOME
$ _____

DECIDE HOW YOU WILL ACTUALLY SPEND THAT MONEY AND GO DO IT. WRITE YOUR REFLECTIONS/LEARNINGS HERE:

WHAT IS ENOUGH?

FOR MY PHYSICAL WELLNESS, ENOUGH MEANS...

FOR MY FINANCIAL WELLNESS, ENOUGH MEANS...

FOR MY SOCIAL WELLNESS, ENOUGH MEANS...

FOR MY SPIRITUAL WELLNESS, ENOUGH MEANS...

FOR ECOLOGICAL WELLNESS, ENOUGH MEANS...

I NOTICE

I WONDER

WEEK 47

REVIEW YOUR FINANCIAL PICTURE FOR THE COMING YEAR.
DECIDE HOW MUCH YOU WILL PLEDGE TO THE MINISTRIES OF
YOUR CHURCH. CONSIDER A 10% TITHE IF YOU ARE BRAVE.

NAME A MINISTRY ABOUT WHICH YOU ARE PASSIONATE. IN WHAT WAY
CAN YOU RAISE MONEY TO SUPPORT IT? FROM WHOM? HOW MUCH?

NAME A BUSINESS THAT IS FOSTERING WELLNESS IN YOUR
COMMUNITY. IN WHAT WAYS CAN YOU SUPPORT THAT BUSINESS WITH
YOUR MONEY?

NAME SOME OF THE NON-PROFIT ORGANIZATIONS THAT ARE
FOSTERING WELLNESS, TRUTH AND RELATIONSHIP IN YOUR
COMMUNITY. IN WHAT WAYS CAN YOU SUPPORT THESE
ORGANIZATIONS WITH YOUR MONEY?

COMPLETE THE PLEDGE CARD ON THIS PAGE. FIND AN ACCOUNTABLE PERSON TO SIGN IT. TAKE A PHOTO AND SEND IT TO SOMEONE WHO OVERSEES STEWARDSHIP MINISTRY IN YOUR CHURCH.

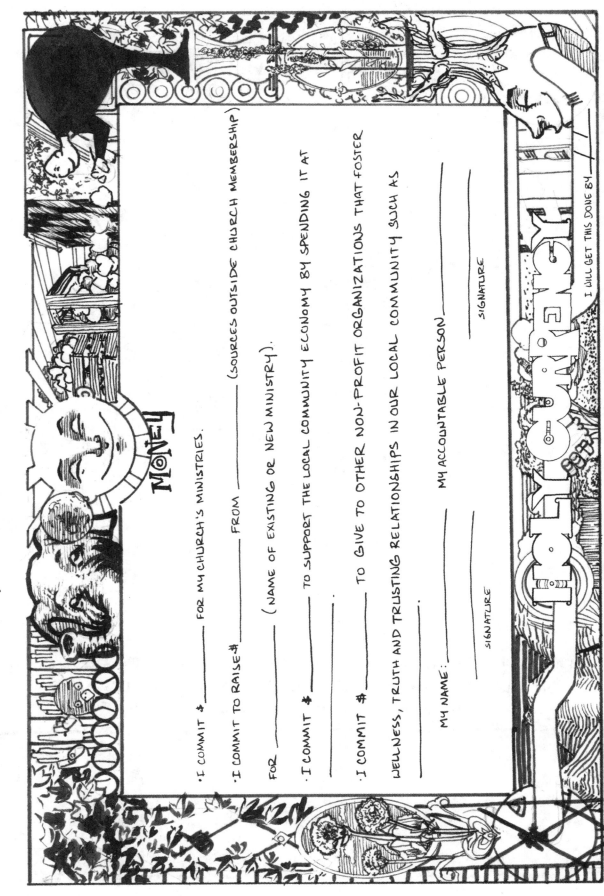

MONEY

HOLY CURRENCY!

• I COMMIT $ _____ FOR MY CHURCH'S MINISTRIES.

• I COMMIT TO RAISE $ _____ FROM _____ (SOURCES OUTSIDE CHURCH MEMBERSHIP)

FOR _____ (NAME OF EXISTING OR NEW MINISTRY).

• I COMMIT $ _____ TO SUPPORT THE LOCAL COMMUNITY ECONOMY BY SPENDING IT AT _____.

• I COMMIT $ _____ TO GIVE TO OTHER NON-PROFIT ORGANIZATIONS THAT FOSTER WELLNESS, TRUTH AND TRUSTING RELATIONSHIPS IN OUR LOCAL COMMUNITY SUCH AS _____.

MY NAME: _____

_____
SIGNATURE

MY ACCOUNTABLE PERSON _____

_____
SIGNATURE

I WILL GET THIS DONE BY _____

ECOLOGICAL WELLNESS

WRITE IN THE CIRCLES ABOVE PEOPLE AND GROUPS IN MY
COMMUNITY THAT CONTRIBUTE TO THE ECOLOGICAL
WELLNESS OF OUR MOTHER EARTH.

STRENGTHS	WEAKNESSES	NEEDS	TO DO

FIND A BABY THIS WEEK.

HOLD THE BABY (IF THE MOTHER WILL LET YOU)

TAKE A PHOTO (IF THE MOTHER WILL LET YOU)

GLUE, TAPE, OR DRAW A PICTURE
OF THE BABY HERE:

WHAT DOES A BABY CALL YOU TO DO IN ORDER TO CREATE A
SUSTAINABLE FUTURE?
· AT HOME?

· AT CHURCH?

· IN YOUR COMMUNITY?

· FOR THE NATION?

· FOR THE EARTH?

WRITE A PRAYER FOR THIS BABY AND FIND A CREATIVE
WAY TO SHARE THE PRAYER WITH THE BABY'S FAMILY.

MEDITATE ON LUKE 2:1-20   MERRY CHRISTMAS!

WEEK 49

LIST THE SABBATICAL ACTIVITIES THAT WOULD INCREASE YOUR PHYSICAL, SOCIAL AND SPIRITUAL WELLNESS:

FOR ME	PHYSICAL WELLNESS	SOCIAL WELLNESS	SPIRITUAL WELLNESS
DAILY			
WEEKLY			
MONTHLY			
ANNUALLY			

LIST THE SABBATICAL ACTIVITIES THAT WOULD INCREASE MY FRIENDS' AND FAMILY'S PHYSICAL, SOCIAL AND SPIRITUAL WELLNESS:

FOR MY FAMILY AND FRIENDS	PHYSICAL WELLNESS	SOCIAL WELLNESS	SPIRITUAL WELLNESS
DAILY			
WEEKLY			
MONTHLY			
ANNUALLY			

LIST THE SABBATICAL ACTIVITIES THAT WOULD INCREASE PHYSICAL, SOCIAL AND SPIRITUAL WELLNESS OF THE PEOPLE IN MY NEIGHBORHOOD COMMUNITY:

FOR MY COMMUNITY	PHYSICAL WELLNESS	SOCIAL WELLNESS	SPIRITUAL WELLNESS
DAILY			
WEEKLY			
MONTHLY			
ANNUALLY			

LIST THE ACTIVITIES THAT WOULD INCREASE THE ECOLOGICAL WELLNESS OF MY NEIGHBORHOOD, TOWN/CITY OR COUNTRY:

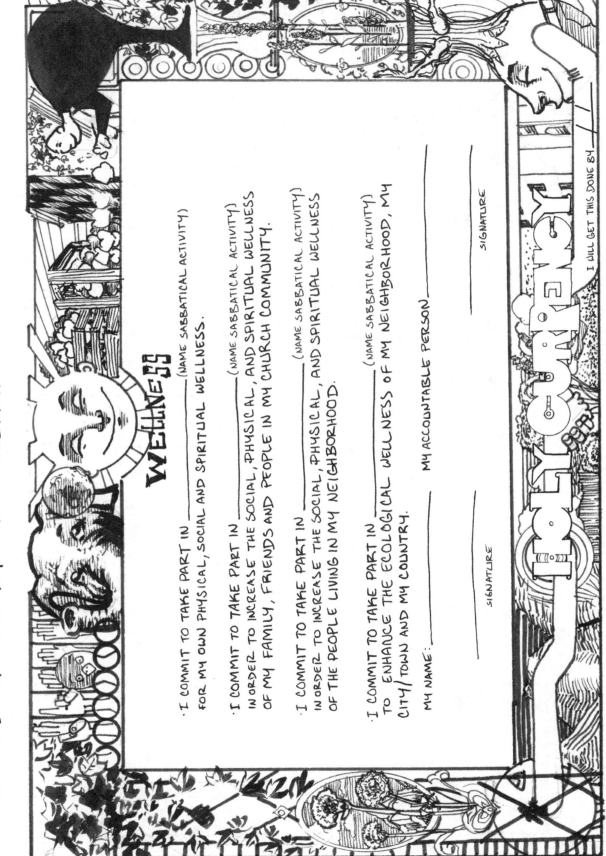

COMPLETE THE PLEDGE CARD ON THIS PAGE. FIND AN ACCOUNTABLE PERSON TO SIGN IT. TAKE A PHOTO AND SEND IT TO SOMEONE WHO OVERSEES STEWARDSHIP MINISTRY IN YOUR CHURCH.

WELLNESS

· I COMMIT TO TAKE PART IN _____ (NAME SABBATICAL ACTIVITY) FOR MY OWN PHYSICAL, SOCIAL AND SPIRITUAL WELLNESS.

· I COMMIT TO TAKE PART IN _____ (NAME SABBATICAL ACTIVITY) IN ORDER TO INCREASE THE SOCIAL, PHYSICAL, AND SPIRITUAL WELLNESS OF MY FAMILY, FRIENDS AND PEOPLE IN MY CHURCH COMMUNITY.

· I COMMIT TO TAKE PART IN _____ (NAME SABBATICAL ACTIVITY) IN ORDER TO INCREASE THE SOCIAL, PHYSICAL, AND SPIRITUAL WELLNESS OF THE PEOPLE LIVING IN MY NEIGHBORHOOD.

· I COMMIT TO TAKE PART IN _____ (NAME SABBATICAL ACTIVITY) TO ENHANCE THE ECOLOGICAL WELLNESS OF MY NEIGHBORHOOD, MY CITY/TOWN AND MY COUNTRY.

MY NAME: _____

SIGNATURE

MY ACCOUNTABLE PERSON _____

SIGNATURE

HOLY CURRENCY

I WILL GET THIS DONE BY _____

I RECEIVE _____

I TAKE IN _____

I MAKE _____

I KEEP _____

I OWN _____

I CONTROL _____

I POSSESS _____

I HOLD _____

I PRODUCE _____

I GENERATE _____

I NOTICE...	I WONDER...

I GIVE _____

I OFFER _____

I TURN OVER _____

I GIVE BACK _____

I DONATE _____

I CONTRIBUTE _____

I LET GO _____

I YIELD _____

I GRANT _____

I RETURN _____

I PASS ON _____

I IMPART _____

I SACRIFICE _____

I NOTICE...

I WONDER...

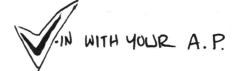 ·IN WITH YOUR A.P.

WEEK 51

REVIEW THIS PAST YEAR AND RECALL AN EVENT OF BLESSING OR TRANSFORMATION FOR YOU.

WRITE DOWN THE SEQUENCE OF EVENTS LEADING TO THIS BLESSING OR TRANSFORMATION (OR DRAW THEM).

NAME THE PERSONS OR GROUPS WHO FACILITATED THIS TRANSFORMATION. DESCRIBE THEIR ACTIONS.

WHAT IS A SYMBOLIC ACTION THAT CAN HELP YOU REMEMBER THIS EVENT? (I.E. DRAW A PICTURE, WRITE A POEM, WRITE A THANK YOU NOTE, OFFER A GIFT, INVITE SOMEONE FOR A MEAL, CREATE A VIDEO, MAKE A PUBLIC STATEMENT, ETC.)

RENEW A PROMISE:
IN THANKSGIVING FOR THE BLESSINGS I RECEIVED THIS PAST YEAR, I PROMISE TO...

FIND AND LISTEN TO THE SONG OFFER TO GOD A SACRIFICE BY ERIC H.F. LAW (WWW.HOLYCURRENCIES.COM) AND DANCE.

OFFER TO GOD A SACRIFICE OF THANKSGIVING AND PAY YOUR VOWS TO THE MOST HIGH.

(PSALM 50:14 NRSV)

YOU HAVE MADE IT TO THE END OF THIS BOOK.

GO BACK TO THE FIRST PAGE AND REVIEW THE HOPE-FOR EXCHANGES FOR DOING THIS BOOK. WERE YOUR HOPES FULFILLED?

LIST ANY ADDITIONAL UNEXPECTED EXCHANGES HERE:

WHAT WILL YOU DO TO GIVE THANKS FOR THE BLESSINGS YOU HAVE RECEIVED THROUGH WORKING ON THIS BOOK?

FIND AND LISTEN TO THE SONG CYCLE OF BLESSINGS BY ERIC H.F. LAW
(WWW. HOLYCURRENCIES.COM) AND DANCE.

WE INVITE YOU TO KEEP THE CYCLE OF BLESSINGS TURNING.

NOW MAKE A PLAN FOR NEXT YEAR!

INDEX

BIBLICAL REFERENCES

WEEK 5 .... MATTHEW 10:29-31
           LUKE 3:21-22

WEEK 7 .... DEUTERONOMY 5:13-14
           DEUTERONOMY 15:1-2
           EXODUS 23:10
           LEVITICUS 24:10-12

WEEK 9 .... PHILIPPIANS 4:12-13

WEEK 14 .... MATTHEW 20:16

WEEK 17 .... ECCLESIASTES 3:1-8

WEEK 21 .... LUKE 10:38-42

WEEK 27 .... MATTHEW 5:44-45

WEEK 28 .... ROMANS 8:16-17

WEEK 29 .... JOHN 14:6

WEEK 33 .... LUKE 6:20-26

WEEK 34 .... EPHESIANS 4:14-16

WEEK 48 .... LUKE 2:1-20

WEEK 51 .... PSALM 50:14

WEEK 52 .... ISAIAH 55:10-11

PLEDGE CARDS:

GRACIOUS LEADERSHIP .... WEEK 16

TIME 19

RELATIONSHIP 24

TRUTH 30

PLACE 40

MONEY 47

ACKNOWLEDGMENTS

TO THE INDIVIDUALS AND CHURCHES THAT HAVE EMBRACED HOLY CURRENCIES: A MODEL OF MINISTRY IS WORTH NOTHING UNLESS IT IS EMBODIED BY REAL ACTIONS, EXPERIENCES AND MINISTRIES. THANK YOU FOR MAKING HOLY CURRENCIES FLOW IN YOUR COMMUNITIES.

TO BRAD LYONS AND THE COURAGEOUS PEOPLE AT CHALICE PRESS: THANK YOU FOR TAKING A CHANCE ON THIS BOOK, WHICH GOES WHERE NO THEOLOGICAL BOOK HAS GONE BEFORE.

TO STEVE RUTBERG AND BECKY LAW: YOUR PATIENCE AND UNDERSTANDING ARE THE GREATEST GIFTS TO TWO OBSESSIVE ARTISTS CREATING.

TO STEPHEN AND LYNN LAW: YOUR SUPPORT AND CONFIDENCE IN US AND THIS BOOK IS UNMATCHED.